The FIRST 100 CHINESE CHARACTERS

The quick and easy way to learn the basic Chinese characters

TRADITIONAL CHARACTER EDITION

Introduction by
Alison and Laurence Matthews

TUTTLE Publishing

Tokyo | Rutland, Vermont | Singapore

ABOUT TUTTLE
"Books to Span the East and West"

Our core mission at Tuttle Publishing is to create books which bring people together one page at a time. Tuttle was founded in 1832 in the small New England town of Rutland, Vermont (USA). Our fundamental values remain as strong today as they were then—to publish best-in-class books informing the English-speaking world about the countries and peoples of Asia. The world has become a smaller place today and Asia's economic, cultural and political influence has expanded, yet the need for meaningful dialogue and information about this diverse region has never been greater. Since 1948, Tuttle has been a leader in publishing books on the cultures, arts, cuisines, languages and literatures of Asia. Our authors and photographers have won numerous awards and Tuttle has published thousands of books on subjects ranging from martial arts to paper crafts. We welcome you to explore the wealth of information available on Asia at **www.tuttlepublishing.com**.

Published by Tuttle Publishing, an imprint of Periplus Editions (HK) Ltd.

www.tuttlepublishing.com

© 2006 by Periplus Editions (HK) Ltd.
All rights reserved.

ISBN 978-0-8048-4492-5

Distributed by:

North America, Latin America & Europe
Tuttle Publishing
364 Innovation Drive North Clarendon, VT 05759-9436
Tel: 1 (802) 773 8930; Fax: 1 (802) 773 6993
info@tuttlepublishing.com
www.tuttlepublishing.com

Japan
Tuttle Publishing
Yaekari Building 3F
5-4-12 Osaki, Shinagawa-ku Tokyo 141-0032, Japan
Tel: (81) 3 5437 0171; Fax: (81) 3 5437 0755
sales@tuttle.co.jp
www.tuttle.co.jp

Asia-Pacific
Berkeley Books Pte Ltd
61 Tai Seng Avenue #02-12 Singapore 534167
Tel: (65) 6280-1330; Fax: (65) 6280-6290
inquiries@periplus.com.sg
www.periplus.com

20 19 18 17   10 9 8 7 6 5 4   1710RR
Printed in China

TUTTLE PUBLISHING® is a registered trademark of Tuttle Publishing, a division of Periplus Editions (HK) Ltd.

Contents

Introduction

Learning the characters is one of the most fascinating and fun parts of learning Chinese, and people are often surprised by how much they enjoy being able to recognize them and to write them. Added to that, *writing* the characters is also the best way of *learning* them. This book shows you how to write the second 100 most common characters and gives you plenty of space to practice writing them. When you do this, you'll be learning a writing system which is one of the oldest in the world and is now used by more than a billion people around the globe every day.

In this introduction we'll talk about:
- how the characters developed;
- the difference between traditional and simplified forms of the characters;
- what the "radicals" are and why they're useful;
- how to count the writing strokes used to form each character;
- how to look up the characters in a dictionary;
- how words are created by joining two characters together; and, most importantly;
- how to write the characters!

Also, in case you're using this book on your own without a teacher, we'll tell you how to get the most out of using it.

Chinese characters are not nearly as strange and complicated as people seem to think. They're actually no more mysterious than musical notation, which most people can master in only a few months. So there's really nothing to be scared of or worried about: everyone can learn them—it just requires a bit of patience and perseverance. There are also some things which you may have heard about writing Chinese characters that aren't true. In particular, you don't need to use a special brush to write them (a ball-point pen is fine), and you don't need to be good at drawing (in fact you don't even need to have neat handwriting, although it helps!).

How many characters are there?
Thousands! You would probably need to know something like two thousand to be able to read Chinese newspapers and books, but you don't need anything like that number to read a menu, go shopping or read simple street signs and instructions. Just as you can get by in most countries knowing about a hundred words of the local language, so too you can get by in China quite well knowing a hundred common Chinese characters. And this would also be an excellent basis for learning to read and write Chinese.

How did the characters originally develop?
Chinese characters started out as pictures representing simple objects, and the first characters originally resembled the things they represented. For example:

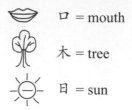

Some other simple characters were pictures of "ideas":

一 one   二 two   三 three

Some of these characters kept this "pictographic" or "ideographic" quality about them, but others were gradually modified or abbreviated until many of them now look nothing like the original objects or ideas.

Then, as words were needed for things which weren't easy to draw, existing characters were "combined" to create new characters. For example, 女 (meaning "woman") combined with 子 (meaning "child") gives a new character 好 (which means "good" or "to be fond of").

Notice that when two characters are joined together like this to form a new character, they get squashed together and deformed slightly. This is so that the new, combined character will fit into the same size square or "box" as each of the original two characters. For example the character 日 "sun" becomes thinner when it is the left-hand part of the character 時 "time"; and it becomes shorter when it is the upper part of the character 星 "star". Some components got distorted and deformed even more than this in the combining process: for example when the character 人 "man" appears on the left-hand side of a complex character it gets compressed into 亻, like in the character 他 "he".

So you can see that some of the simpler characters often act as basic "building blocks" from which more complex characters are formed. This means that if you learn how to write these simple characters you'll also be learning how to write some complex ones too.

How are characters read and pronounced?

The pronunciations in this workbook refer to modern standard Chinese. This is the official language of China and is also known as "Mandarin" or "**putonghua**".

The pronunciation of Chinese characters is written out with letters of the alphabet using a romanization system called "Hanyu Pinyin"—or "**pinyin**" for short. This is the modern system used in China. In pinyin some of the letters have a different sound than in English—but if you are learning Chinese you'll already know this. We could give a description here of how to pronounce each sound, but it would take up a lot of space—and this workbook is about writing the characters, not pronouncing them! In any case, you really need to hear a teacher (or recording) pronounce the sounds out loud to get an accurate idea of what they sound like.

Each Chinese character is pronounced using only one syllable. However, in addition to the syllable, each character also has a particular *tone*, which refers to how the pitch of the voice is used. In standard Chinese there are four different tones, and in pinyin the tone is marked by placing an accent mark over the vowel as follows:

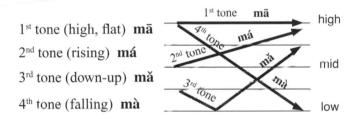

1st tone (high, flat) **mā**

2nd tone (rising) **má**

3rd tone (down-up) **mǎ**

4th tone (falling) **mà**

The pronunciation of each character is therefore a combination of a syllable and a tone. There are only a small number of available syllables in Chinese, and many characters therefore share the same syllable—in fact many characters share the same sound plus tone combination. They are like the English words "here" and "hear"—when they are spoken, you can only tell which is which from the context or by seeing the word in written form.

Apart from **putonghua** (modern standard Chinese), another well-known type of Chinese is Cantonese, which is spoken in southern China and in many Chinese communities around the world. In fact there are several dozen different Chinese languages, and the pronunciations of Chinese characters in these languages are all very different from each other. But the important thing to realize is that the characters themselves do *not* change. So two Chinese people who can't understand each other when they're talking together, can write to one another without any problem at all!

Simplified and traditional characters

As more and more characters were introduced over the years by combining existing characters, some of them became quite complicated. Writing them required many strokes which was time-consuming, and it became difficult to distinguish some of them, especially when the writing was small. So when writing the characters quickly in hand-written form, many people developed short-cuts and wrote them in a more simplified form. In the middle of the 20th century, the Chinese decided to create a standardised set of simplified characters to be used by everyone in China. This resulted in many of the more complicated characters being given simplified forms, making them much easier to learn and to write. Today in China, and also in Singapore, these simplified characters are used almost exclusively, and many Chinese no longer learn the old traditional forms. However the full traditional forms continue to be used in Taiwan and in overseas Chinese communities around the world.

Here are some examples of how some characters were simplified:

Traditional		Simplified
見	→	见
飯	→	饭
號	→	号
幾	→	几

Modern standard Chinese uses only simplified characters. But it is useful to be able to recognize the traditional forms as they are still used in many places outside China, and of course older books and inscriptions were also written using the traditional forms. This workbook teaches the full traditional forms. If there is a simplified form, then it is shown in a separate box on the right-hand side of the page so that you can see what it looks like.

How is Chinese written?

Chinese was traditionally written from top to bottom in columns beginning on the right-hand side of the page and working towards the left, like this:

幸福一點兒也不
難擁有。祇要妳
常為人着想，帶
來歡樂，妳會發
覺到那也是一種
幸福呀！

This means that for a book printed in this way, you start by opening it at (what Westerners would think of as) the back cover. While writing in columns is sometimes considered archaic, you will still find many books, especially novels and more serious works of history, printed in this way.

Nowadays, though, most Chinese people write from left to right in horizontal lines working from the top of a page to the bottom, just as we do in English.

Are Chinese characters the same as English words?
Although each character has a meaning, it's not really true that an individual character is equivalent to an English "word". Each character is actually only a single *syllable*. In Chinese (like in English) some words are just one syllable, but most words are made up of two or more syllables joined together. The vast majority of words in Chinese actually consist of two separate characters placed together in a pair. These multi-syllable words are often referred to as "compounds", and this workbook provides a list of common compounds for each character.

Some Chinese characters are one-syllable words on their own (like the English words "if" and "you"), while other characters are only ever used as one half of a word (like the English syllables "sen" and "tence"). Some characters do both: they're like the English "light" which is happy as a word on its own, but which also links up to form words like "headlight" or "lighthouse".

The Chinese write sentences by stringing characters together in a long line from left to right (or in a column from top to bottom), with equal-sized spaces between each character. If English were written this way—as individual syllables rather than as words that are joined together—it would mean all the syllables would be written separately with spaces in between them, something like this:

If you can un der stand this sen tence you can read Chi nese too.

So in theory, you can't see which characters are paired together to form words, but in practice, once you know a bit of Chinese, you can!

Punctuation was not traditionally used when writing Chinese, but today commas, periods (full stops), quotation marks, and exclamation points are all used along with other types of punctuation which have been borrowed from English.

Two ways of putting characters together
We have looked at *combining characters* together to make new *characters*, and *pairing characters* together to make *words*. So what's the difference?

Well, when two *simple characters* are combined to form a new *complex character*, they are squashed or distorted so that the new character fits into the same size square as the original characters. The meaning of the new character *may* be related to the meaning of its components, but it frequently appears to have no connection with them at all! The new complex character also has a new single-syllable pronunciation, which may or may not be related to the pronunciation of one of its parts. For example:

女	+	也	=	她
nǚ		**yě**		**tā**
woman		also		she

日	+	月	=	明
rì		**yuè**		**míng**
sun		moon/month		bright

On the other hand, when characters are *paired together* to create *words*, the characters are simply written one after the other, normal sized, with a normal space in between (and there are no hyphens or anything to show that these characters are working together as a pair). The resulting word has a pronunciation which is *two* syllables—it is simply the pronunciations of the two individual characters one after the other. Also, you're much more likely to be able to guess the meaning of the word from the meanings of the individual characters that make it up. For example:

大	+	人	=	大人
dà		**rén**		**dà rén**
big		person		adult

姐	+	妹	=	姐妹
jiě		**mèi**		**jiě mèi**
older sister		younger sister		sisters

四	+	月	=	四月
sì		**yuè**		**sì yuè**
four		moon/month		April

再	+	見	=	再見
zài		**jiàn**		**zài jiàn**
again		see; meet		Goodbye!

Is it necessary to learn words as well as characters?
As we've said, the meaning of a compound word is often related to the meanings of the individual characters. But this is not always the case, and sometimes the word takes on a new and very specific meaning. So to be able to read Chinese sentences and understand what they mean, it isn't enough just to learn individual characters—you'll also need to learn words. (In fact, many individual characters have very little meaning at all by themselves, and only take on meanings when paired with other characters).

Here are some examples of common Chinese words where the meaning of the overall word is not what you might expect from the meanings of the individual characters:

明		天		明天
míng	**+**	**tiān**	**=**	**míng tiān**
bright		day/sky		tomorrow

好		在		好在
hǎo	**+**	**zài**	**=**	**hǎo zài**
good		be present at/ live at		fortunately

If you think about it, the same thing happens in English. If you know what "battle" and "ship" mean, you can probably guess what a "battleship" might be. But this wouldn't work with "championship"! Similarly, you'd be unlikely to guess the meaning of "honeymoon" if you only knew the words "honey" and "moon".

The good news is that learning compound words can help you to learn the characters. For example, you may know (from your Chinese lessons) that **xīng qī** means "week". So when you see that this word is written 星期, you will know that 星 is pronounced **xīng**, and 期 is pronounced **qī**—even when these characters are forming part of *other* words. In fact, you will find that you remember many characters as half of some familiar word.

When you see a word written in characters, you can also often see how the word came to mean what it does. For example, **xīng qī** is 星期 which literally means "star period". This will help you to remember both the word *and* the two individual characters.

What is a stroke count?
Each Chinese character is made up of a number of pen or brush strokes. Each individual stroke is the mark made by a pen or brush before lifting it off the paper to write the next stroke. Strokes come in various shapes and sizes—a stroke can be a straight line, a curve, a bent line, a line with

a hook, or a dot. There is a traditional and very specific way that every character should be written. The order and direction of the strokes are both important if the character is to have the correct appearance.

What counts as a stroke is determined by tradition and is not always obvious. For example, the small box that often appears as part of a character (like the one on page 32, in the character 名) counts as three strokes, not four! (This is because a single stroke is traditionally used to write the top and right-hand sides of the box).

All this may sound rather pedantic but it is well worth learning how to write the characters correctly and with the correct number of strokes. One reason is that knowing how to count the strokes correctly is useful for looking up characters in dictionaries, as you'll see later.

This book shows you how to write characters stroke by stroke, and once you get the feel of it you'll very quickly learn how to work out the stroke count of a character you haven't met before, and get it right!

What are radicals?
Although the earliest characters were simple drawings, most characters are complex with two or more parts. And you'll find that some simple characters appear over and over again as parts of many complex characters. Have a look at these five characters:

她	she
媽	mother
姐	older sister
好	good
姓	surname

All five of these characters have the same component on the left-hand side: 女, which means "woman". This component gives a clue to the meaning of the character, and is called the "radical". As you can see, most of these five characters have something to do with the idea of "woman", but as you can also see, it's not a totally reliable way of guessing the meaning of a character. (Meanings of characters are something you just have to learn, without much help from their component parts).

Unfortunately the radical isn't always on the left-hand side of a character. Sometimes it's on the right, or on the top, or on the bottom. Here are some examples:

Character	Radical	Position of radical
都	阝	right
星	日	top
您	心	bottom
這	辶	left and bottom

Because it's not always easy to tell what the radical is for a particular character, it's given explicitly in a separate box for each of the characters in this book. However, as you learn more and more characters, you'll find that you can often guess the radical just by looking at a character.

Why bother with radicals? Well, for hundreds of years Chinese dictionaries have used the radical component of each character as a way of indexing them. All characters, even the really simple ones, are assigned to one radical or another so that they can be placed within the index of a Chinese dictionary (see the next section).

Incidentally, when you take away the radical, what's left is often a clue to the *pronunciation* of the character (this remainder is called the "phonetic component"). For example, 嗎 and 媽 are formed by adding different radicals to the character 馬 "horse" which is pronounced **mǎ**. Now 嗎 is pronounced **ma** and 媽 is pronounced **mā**, so you can see that these two characters have inherited their pronunciations from the phonetic component 馬. Unfortunately these "phonetic components" aren't very dependable: for example 也 on its own is pronounced **yě** but 他 and 她 are both pronounced **tā**.

How do I find a character in an index or a dictionary?
This is a question lots of people ask, and the answer varies according to the type of dictionary you are using. Many dictionaries today are organized alphabetically by pronunciation. So if you want to look up a character in a dictionary and you know its pronunciation, then it's easy. It's when you don't know the pronunciation of a character that there's a problem, since there is no alphabetical order for characters like there is for English words.

If you don't know the pronunciation of a character, then you will need to use a radical index (which is why radicals are useful). To use this you have to know which part of the character is the radical, and you will also need to be able to count the number of strokes that make up the character. To look up 姓, for example, 女 is the radical (which has 3 strokes) and the remaining part 生 has 5 strokes. So first you find the radical 女 amongst the 3-stroke radicals in the radical index. Then, since there are lots of characters under 女, look for 姓 in the section which lists all the 女 characters which have 5-stroke remainders.

This workbook has both a Hanyu Pinyin index and a radical index. Why not get used to how these indexes work by picking a character in the book and seeing if you can find it in both of the indexes?

Many dictionaries also have a pure stroke count index (i.e. ignoring the radical). This is useful if you cannot figure out what the radical of the character is. To use this you must count up all the strokes in the character as a whole and then look the character up under that number (so you would look up 姓 under 8 strokes). As you can imagine, this type of index can leave you with long columns of characters to scan through before you find the one you're looking for, so it's usually a last resort!

All these methods have their pitfalls and complications, so recently a completely new way of looking up characters has been devised. The *Chinese Character Fast Finder* (also by Tuttle Publishing) organizes characters purely by their shapes so that you can look up any one of 3,000 characters very quickly without knowing its meaning, radical, pronunciation or stroke count!

How should I use this workbook?
One good way to learn characters is to practice writing them, especially if you think about what each character means as you write it. This will fix the characters in your memory better than if you just look at them without writing them.

If you're working on your own without a teacher, work on a few characters at a time. Go at a pace that suits you; it's much better to do small but regular amounts of writing than to do large chunks at irregular intervals. You might start with just one or two characters each day and increase this as you get better at it. Frequent repetition is the key! Try to get into a daily routine of learning a few new characters and also reviewing the ones you learned on previous days. It's also a good idea to keep a list of which characters you've learned each day, and then to "test yourself" on the characters you learned the previous day, three days ago, a week ago and a month ago. Each time you test yourself they will stay in your memory for a longer period.

But *don't* worry if you can't remember a character you wrote out ten times only yesterday! This is quite normal to begin with. Just keep going—it will all be sinking in without you realizing it.

Once you've learned a few characters you can use flash cards to test yourself on them in a random order. You can make your own set of cards, or use a ready-made set like Tuttle's *Chinese Flash Cards*.

How do I write the characters?
Finally, let's get down to business and talk about actually writing the characters! Under each character in this book, the first few boxes show how the character is written, stroke by stroke. There is a correct way to draw each

character, and the diagrams in the boxes show you both the order to draw the strokes in, and also the direction for each stroke.

Use the three gray examples to trace over and then carry on by yourself, drawing the characters using the correct stroke order and directions. The varying thicknesses of the lines show you what the characters would look like if they were drawn with a brush, but if you're using a pencil or ball-point pen don't worry about this. Just trace down the middle of the lines and you will produce good hand-written characters.

Pay attention to the length of each of the strokes so that your finished character has the correct proportions. Use the gray dotted lines inside each box as a guide to help you start and end each stroke in the right place.

You may think that it doesn't really matter how the strokes are written as long as the end result looks the same. To some extent this is true, but there are some good reasons for knowing the "proper" way to write the characters. Firstly, it helps you to count strokes, and secondly it will make your finished character "look right", and also help you to read other people's hand-written characters later on. It's better in the long run to learn the correct method of writing the characters from the beginning because, as with so many other things, once you get into "bad" habits it can be very hard to break them!

If you are left-handed, just use your left hand as normal, but still make sure you use the correct stroke order and directions when writing the strokes. For example, draw your horizontal strokes left to right, even if it feels more natural to draw them right to left.

For each Chinese character there is a fixed, correct order in which to write the strokes. But these "stroke orders" do follow some fairly general rules. The main thing to remember is:

- Generally work left to right and top to bottom.

Some other useful guidelines are:
- Horizontal lines are written before vertical ones (see 十, page 19);
- Lines that slope down and to the left are written before those that slope down and to the right (see 文, page 41);
- A central part or vertical line is written before symmetrical or smaller lines at the sides (see 小, page 47);
- The top and sides of an outer box are written first, then whatever is inside the box, then the bottom is written last to "close" it (see 國, page 56).

As you work through the book you'll see these rules in action and get a feel for them, and you'll know how to draw virtually any Chinese character without having to be shown.

Practice, practice, practice!

Your first attempts at writing will be awkward, but as with most things you'll get better with practice. That's why there are lots of squares for you to use. And don't be too hard on yourself (we all draw clumsy-looking characters when we start); just give yourself plenty of time and practice. After a while, you'll be able to look back at your early attempts and compare them with your most recent ones, and see just how much you've improved.

After writing the same character a number of times (a row or two at most), move on to another one. Don't fill up the whole page at one sitting! Then, after writing several other characters, come back later and do a few more of the first one. Can you remember the stroke order without having to look at the diagram?

Finally, try writing out sentences, or lines of different characters, on ordinary paper. To begin with you can mark out squares to write in if you want to, but after that simply imagine the squares and try to keep your characters all equally sized and equally spaced.

Have fun, and remember—the more you practice writing the characters the easier it gets!

一

yī one; single; a(n)

common words

一個　**yí ge**　a(n); one (of something)
一次　**yí cì**　once
一同／一起　**yī tóng/yī qǐ**　together
一月　**yí yuè**　January
十一　**shí yī**　eleven
第一　**dì yī**　first
星期一　**xīng qī yī**　Monday

1 stroke

radical

一

二 **èr** two (number)	**common words** 二十 **èr shí** twenty 二妹 **èr mèi** second younger sister 二月 **èr yuè** February 二手 **èr shǒu** secondhand (adj.) 十二 **shí èr** twelve 第二 **dì èr** second (sequence) 星期二 **xīng qī èr** Tuesday	**2 strokes** **radical** 二

三 **sān** three	**common words** 三十 **sān shí** thirty 三月 **sān yuè** March 三個月 **sān ge yuè** three months 三明治 **sān míng zhì** sandwich 十三 **shí sān** thirteen 第三 **dì sān** third 星期三 **xīng qī sān** Wednesday	**3 strokes** **radical** 一

12

四

sì four

common words

四十　**sì shí**　forty
四百　**sì bǎi**　four hundred
四月　**sì yuè**　April
四處　**sì chù**　everywhere
十四　**shí sì**　fourteen
第四　**dì sì**　fourth
星期四　**xīng qī sì**　Thursday

五

wǔ five

common words

五十　**wǔ shí**　fifty
五月　**wǔ yuè**　May
五年　**wǔ nián**　five years
五本　**wǔ běn**　five (books)
十五　**shí wǔ**　fifteen
第五　**dì wǔ**　fifth
星期五　**xīng qī wǔ**　Friday

六

liù six

4 strokes

radical

八

common words

六十三 **liù shí sān** sixty-three
六月 **liù yuè** June
六個月 **liù ge yuè** six months
六天 **liù tiān** six days
十六 **shí liù** sixteen
第六 **dì liù** sixth
星期六 **xīng qī liù** Saturday

丶	亠	六	六	六	六	六

七

qī seven

common words

七十七　**qī shí qī**　seventy-seven
七百　**qī bǎi**　seven hundred
七月　**qī yuè**　July
十七　**shí qī**　seventeen
七七八八　**qī qī bā bā**　almost complete
七上八下　**qī shàng bā xià**　worry; anxious
第七　**dì qī**　seventh

一　七　七　七　七

八	**common words**	**2 strokes**
	八十二 **bā shí èr** eighty-two	**radical**
	八百零五 **bā bǎi líng wǔ** eight-hundred and five	八
	八月 **bā yuè** August	
	八成 **bā chéng** 80 per cent	
	八折 **bā zhé** 20 per cent discount	
bā eight	十八 **shí bā** eighteen	
	第八 **dì bā** eighth	

八 八 八 八

九

jiǔ nine

common words

九十八　**jiǔ shí bā**　ninety-eight
九百一十　**jiǔ bǎi yí shí**　nine-hundred and ten
九月　**jiǔ yuè**　September
九號　**jiǔ hào**　number/size nine; ninth (of a month)
九分　**jiǔ fēn**　nine points
十九　**shí jiǔ**　nineteen
第九　**dì jiǔ**　ninth

2 strokes

radical

乙

18

十			

shí ten

common words

十月 **shí yuè** October
十一月 **shí yī yuè** November
十二月 **shí èr yuè** December
十分 **shí fēn** 1. ten points 2. very
十全十美 **shí quán shí měi** perfect; ideal
第十 **dì shí** tenth

2 strokes

radical

十

你

nǐ you

radical

人 （ 亻 ）

common words

你好　**nǐ hǎo**　How do you do?
你的　**nǐ de**　your; yours
你們　**nǐ men**　you (plural)
你們的　**nǐ men de**　your; yours (plural)

亻	亻	亻	你	你	你	你	你
你	你						

20

您		

nín you (polite)

您好 **nín hǎo** How do you do? (polite)
您早 **nín zǎo** Good morning!
您貴姓? **nín guì xìng** your family name?

11 strokes

radical

心

21

好

hǎo/hào 1. good
2. alright 3. like

common words

好啊! **hǎo a** Good!; OK!
好看 **hǎo kàn** 1. good show 2. good looking
好久 **hǎo jiǔ** a long time
很好 **hěn hǎo** very good
還好 **hái hǎo** still alright
那好 **nà hǎo** alright then ... (agreeing to a suggestion)
愛好 **ài hào** hobby, interest in something

6 strokes

radical

女

請

qǐng 1. please
2. to invite

common words

請問　qǐng wèn　May I ask ...?
請坐　qǐng zuò　Please sit down.
請進　qǐng jìn　Please come in.
請客　qǐng kè　play host; treat
請教　qǐng jiào　seek advice
請假　qǐng jià　take leave

15 strokes

radical
言

simplified form
请

問

wèn ask

radical
口

simplified form
问

common words

問好 **wèn hǎo** say hello to...
問題 **wèn tí** question; problem
問答 **wèn dá** question and answer
學問 **xué wèn** knowledge
訪問 **fǎng wèn** 1. visit 2. interview

貴			

guì 1. honorable
2. expensive; valuable

common words

貴姓 **guì xìng** your honorable surname?
貴人 **guì rén** respected person
貴客/貴賓 **guì kè/guì bīn** distinguished guest; VIP
太貴了 **tài guì le** too expensive
名貴 **míng guì** valuable

12 strokes

radical
貝

simplified form
贵

丶	口	口	中	虫	虫	責	青
青	責	貴	貴	貴	貴	貴	

姓

xìng surname

姓名　**xìng míng**　full name
同姓　**tóng xìng**　having the same surname
老百姓　**lǎo bǎi xìng**　common people

8 strokes

radical

女

⟍	女	女	女	女	女	姓	姓
姓	姓	姓					

他

tā he

common words

他的　**tā de**　his
他們　**tā men**　they; them (male)
他們的　**tā men de**　their; theirs (male)
他人/其他人　**tā rén/qí tā rén**　other people
其他　**qí tā**　other

5 strokes

radical

人（亻）

丿	亻	仍	仦	他	他	他	他

tā she

common words

她的 **tā de** hers
她們 **tā men** they; them (female)
她們的 **tā men de** their; theirs (female)

6 strokes

radical
女

叫

jiào 1. call; be called
2. shout 3. order

common words

叫門　**jiào mén**　call at the door
叫好　**jiào hǎo**　cheer
叫喊　**jiào hǎn**　shout; yell
叫做　**jiào zuò**　be called
叫車　**jiào chē**　order a cab
大叫　**dà jiào**　call out loudly

5 strokes

radical

口

丨	冂	口	叩	叫	叫	叫	叫

什		**common words**		什麼 shén me what		**4 strokes**

什麼 **shén me** what
什麼的 **shén me de** etc; so on...
什麼時候? **shén me shí hòu** when?; at what time?

4 strokes

radical

人（亻）

shén/shí 1. mixed
2. tenth (mathematics)

ノ	亻	仁	什	什	什	什	

麼

me interrogative particle

common words

什麼 **shén me** what
怎麼 **zěn me** how
那麼 **nà me** in that way; so...
多麼 **duō me** no matter how
為什麼? **wèi shén me** why?

名

míng 1. name
2. fame

common words

名字　**míng zi**　name
名叫　**míng jiào**　named
名人　**míng rén**　celebrity; famous person
同名　**tóng míng**　having the same name
出名　**chū míng**　become famous; well-known
第一名　**dì yī míng**　first in position

ノ	ク	タ	夕	名	名	名	名
名							

字

zì written character

common words

字母 **zì mǔ** letter (alphabet)
字典 **zì diǎn** dictionary
十字 **shí zì** cross (n.)
漢字 **hàn zì** Chinese (Han) character
寫字 **xiě zì** write word
生字 **shēng zì** new word

6 strokes

radical

子

33

我

wǒ I; me

radical

戈

common words

我的 **wǒ de** my; mine
我們/咱們 **wǒ men/zán men** we; us
我國 **wǒ guó** our country
我家 **wǒ jiā** my family; my home
自我 **zì wǒ** self

是

shì to be; yes

radical

日

common words

是的 **shì de** yes
是啊 **shì a** yes; yeah
是不是 **shì bu shì** to be or not to be
不是 **bú shi** 1. not to be; no 2. fault
還是 **hái shì** or
老是 **lǎo shì** always

丨	冂	日	旦	旦	早	导	是

是	是	是	是				

大

dà big; great

common words

大聲點 **dà shēng diǎn** louder
大家 **dà jiā** everybody
大不了 **dà bu liǎo** at the worst
大多/大都/大半 **dà duō/dà dū/dà bàn** mostly
大小 **dà xiǎo** size
大概 **dà gài** probably
自大 **zì dà** proud; arrogant

一 ナ 大 大 大 大

學

xué learn

common words

學會　**xué huì**　learned; mastered
學習　**xué xí**　study
上學　**shàng xué**　go to school
放學　**fàng xué**　finish school for the day
開學　**kāi xué**　school reopens
小學　**xiǎo xué**　primary school
中學　**zhōng xué**　middle/secondary school

16 strokes

radical
子

simplified form
学

生

shēng 1. give birth; born 2. raw

common words

生日　**shēng rì**　birthday
生氣　**shēng qì**　angry
生病　**shēng bìng**　fall sick; not well
生吃　**shēng chī**　eat raw food
學生　**xué sheng**　student
先生　**xiān sheng**　1. Mr 2. husband
醫生　**yī shēng**　doctor

5 strokes

radical

生

丿	仁	仁	牛	生	生	生	生

38

中

zhōng/zhòng 1. among
2. (in the) course 3. hit by

common words

中國 **zhōng guó** China
中文 **zhōng wén** Chinese language (written)
中間 **zhōng jiān** between; in the middle
中年 **zhōng nián** middle-aged
中獎 **zhòng jiǎng** win a prize
心中 **xīn zhōng** in one's heart
手中 **shǒu zhōng** on hand

4 strokes

radical

丨

丨 口 口 中 中 中 中

英

yīng 1. related to England 2. hero

英國	**yīng guó**	England
英文	**yīng wén**	English language (written)
英語	**yīng yǔ**	English language
英俊	**yīng jùn**	handsome
英明	**yīng míng**	wise
英雄	**yīng xióng**	hero

8 strokes

radical

艸（艹）

40

文

wén written language; writing

common words

文字 **wén zì** script; writing
文具 **wén jù** stationery
文學 **wén xué** literature
語文 **yǔ wén** language (spoken and written)
法文 **fǎ wén** French (written)
日文 **rì wén** Japanese (written)

課

kè lesson; class

radical

言

simplified form

课

common words

课本 **kè běn** textbook
课题 **kè tí** topic (of lessons)
课文 **kè wén** text
上课 **shàng kè** attend class
下课 **xià kè** finish class
功课 **gōng kè** homework
第一课 **dì yī kè** first lesson; lesson one

丶	二	三	言	言	言	言	訁
訁	訁	誤	誤	課	課	課	課
課	課						

老

lǎo old

common words

老師　**lǎo shī**　teacher
老大　**lǎo dà**　1. eldest sibling 2. gang leader
老婆　**lǎo po**　wife (informal)
老公　**lǎo gōng**　husband (informal)
老婆婆　**lǎo pó po**　old woman
老外　**lǎo wài**　foreigner
古老　**gǔ lǎo**　ancient

一	十	土	少	耂	老	老	老
老							

師	common words	10 strokes
	師生 **shī shēng** teacher and student	radical
	師父 **shī fu** master	巾
	老師/教師 **lǎo shī/jiào shī** teacher	
	律師 **lǜ shī** lawyer	simplified form
shī teacher; master	廚師 **chú shī** chef	师

ノ¹	亻²	𠂤³	𠂤⁴	𠂤⁵	𠂤⁶	𠂤⁷	𠂤⁸
師⁹	師¹⁰	師	師	師			

同

tóng the same;
together

common words

同學 **tóng xué** classmate
同班 **tóng bān** same class
同時 **tóng shí** at the same time
同樣 **tóng yàng** the same; alike
同事 **tóng shì** colleague
一同／一起 **yī tóng/yī qǐ** together

6 strokes

radical

口

校

xiào school

common words

校長　**xiào zhǎng**　principal
校服　**xiào fú**　school uniform
校友　**xiào yǒu**　schoolmate; alumni
學校　**xué xiào**　school
同校　**tóng xiào**　same school
上校　**shàng xiào**　colonel

一	十	才	木	朮	朾	杧	杧
杧	校	校	校	校			

小

xiǎo small; little

common words

小姐 **xiǎo jiě** Miss; lady
小時 **xiǎo shí** hour
小時候 **xiǎo shí hou** in one's childhood
小心 **xiǎo xīn** (be) careful
小看 **xiǎo kàn** belittle; underestimate
小便 **xiǎo biàn** urine; urinate

3 strokes

radical

小

亅	小	小	小	小	小		

朋

péng friend

朋友 **péng you** friend
好朋友 **hǎo péng you** good friend
男朋友 **nán péng you** boyfriend
女朋友 **nǚ péng you** girlfriend
老朋友 **lǎo péng you** old friend
小朋友 **xiǎo péng you** kid; child

8 strokes

radical

月

丿	月	月	月	朋	朋	朋	朋
朋	朋	朋					

48

友

yǒu friend

common words

友人　**yǒu rén**　friend
友誼／友情　**yǒu yì/yǒu qíng**　friendship
好友　**hǎo yǒu**　good friend
男友　**nán yǒu**　boyfriend
女友　**nǚ yǒu**　girlfriend
工友　**gōng yǒu**　fellow worker; caretaker

4 strokes

radical

又

一　ナ　方　友　友　友　友

們

men plural suffix
(for persons)

common words

你們 **nǐ men** you (plural)
我們/咱們 **wǒ men/zán men** we; us
女士們 **nǚ shì men** ladies
男士們 **nán shì men** gentlemen
同學們 **tóng xué men** classmates
人們 **rén men** people

10 strokes

radical

人（亻）

simplified form

们

呢

ne question particle

common words

你呢? **nǐ ne** How about you?
他（她）呢? **tā ne** How about him (her)?
我們呢? **wǒ men ne** How about us?
人呢? **rén ne** Where's the person?

丨	口	口	呀	吕	呎	呢	呢

呢	呢	呢					

謝

xiè thank

common words

謝謝　**xiè xie**　thank you
謝詞　**xiè cí**　thank you speech
多謝　**duō xiè**　many thanks
不謝　**bú xiè**　don't mention it
答謝　**dá xiè**　express appreciation

17 strokes

radical

言

simplified form

谢

1 丶	2 二	3 三	4 言	5 言	6 言	7 言	8 言
9 訁	10 訁	11 訇	12 諍	13 諍	14 諍	15 諍	16 謝
17 謝	謝	謝	謝				

52

再

zài again

再見/再會 **zài jiàn/zài huì** Goodbye!
再三 **zài sān** again and again; repeatedly
再次 **zài cì** once more
再不 **zài bu** or; or else
一再 **yí zài** again and again; repeatedly
不再 **bú zài** no longer; never again

6 strokes

radical

冂

一 丆 冃 冃 再 再 再 再

再

見

jiàn see; meet

radical

見

simplified form

见

common words

見好 **jiàn hǎo** get better (from an illness)
見面 **jiàn miàn** meet
不見了 **bú jiàn le** missing; can't be found
不見得 **bú jiàn de** not necessarily
看見 **kàn jiàn** see
少見 **shǎo jiàn** rare
聽見 **tīng jiàn** hear

丨¹	冂²	冃³	月⁴	目⁵	貝⁶	見⁷ 見
見 見						

美

měi beautiful

common words

美麗 **měi lì** beautiful; pretty

美好 **měi hǎo** wonderful

美食 **měi shí** culinary delicacy, gourmet food

美女／美人 **měi nǚ／měi rén** beautiful girl/woman

美國 **měi guó** the Unites States of America

很美／太美了 **hěn měi／tài měi le** very beautiful

⼂	⼆	⼆	⼆	⼆	羊	羊	美
美	美	美	美				

國	**common words**	**11 strokes**

國家 **guó jiā** country
國民 **guó mín** people of a country
國王 **guó wáng** king
出國 **chū guó** go abroad
外國 **wài guó** foreign country
外國人 **wài guó rén** people from another country, foreigners

guó country; national

radical
口

simplified form
国

56

人

rén person; people

common words

人人/每人 **rén rén/měi rén** everyone
人口 **rén kǒu** population
工人 **gōng rén** worker
大人/成人 **dà rén/chéng rén** adult
本人 **běn rén** oneself
客人 **kè rén** guest

丿人 人 人 人

嗎

ma question particle

common words

是嗎? **shì ma** Is that so?; Is it?
好嗎? **hǎo ma** good?; alright?
忙嗎? **máng ma** busy?
行嗎? **xíng ma** Is it okay?
可以嗎? **kě yǐ ma** May I?
有事嗎? **yǒu shì ma** what's up?

13 strokes

radical

口

simplified form

吗

丨¹	口²	口³	口⁴	口⁵	口⁶	口⁷	唯⁸
嗎⁹	嗎¹⁰	嗎¹¹	嗎¹²	嗎¹³	嗎	嗎	嗎

58

也

yě also; too

也是 **yě shì** is also ...
也好 **yě hǎo** may as well
也許 **yě xǔ** perhaps

2 strokes

radical

乙

59

不

bù not; no

common words

不對 **bú duì** 1. incorrect 2. something is wrong
不要 **bú yào** don't want
不會 **bú huì** 1. don't know how 2. unlikely
不同/不一樣 **bù tóng/bù yí yàng** it's different
不客氣 **bú kè qi** not at all; don't mention it
不好意思 **bù hǎo yì si** 1. embarrassed 2. excuse me
對不起 **duì bu qǐ** sorry

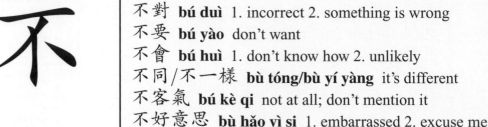

	common words						15 strokes
誰	誰的 **shéi de/shuí de** whose 誰知道 **shéi zhī dào/shuí zhī dào** no one knows						radical 言
shéi/shuí who							simplified form 谁

丶¹	二²	三³	言⁴	言⁵	言⁶	言⁷	訁⁸
訁⁹	訁¹⁰	訁¹¹	訁¹²	誰¹³	誰¹⁴	誰¹⁵	誰
誰	誰						

的

de particle

common words

我的 **wǒ de** my; mine
你的 **nǐ de** your; yours
他的/她的 **tā de** his/hers
誰的 **shéi de/shuí de** whose
有的 **yǒu de** some
挺好的 **tǐng hǎo de** quite good

´¹	⺅²	³白	白⁴	白⁵	的⁶	的⁷	的⁸
的	的	的					

家

jiā family; home

common words

家庭 **jiā tíng** family

家人 **jiā rén** family member

人家 **rén jiā** other people

回家 **huí jiā** return home

每家/家家 **měi jiā/jiā jiā** every family; every household

一家大小 **yī jiā dà xiǎo** everyone in a family

⟍¹	⟍²	宀³	宀⁴	宀⁵	宀⁶	家⁷	家⁸
家⁹	家¹⁰	家	家	家			

爸

bà father

common words

爸爸 **bà ba** father
爸爸媽媽 **bà ba mā ma** parents
老爸 **lǎo bà** father (informal)

8 strokes

radical
父

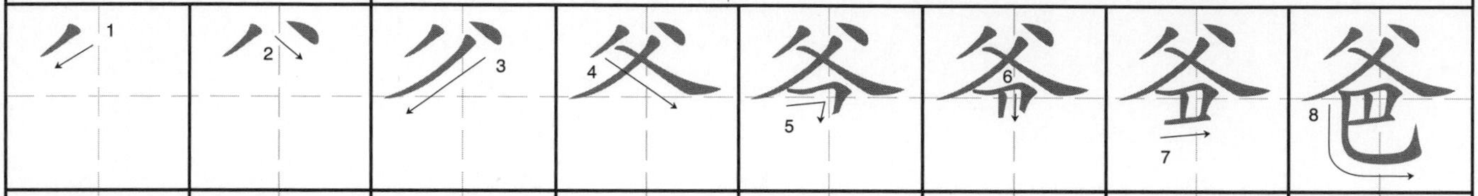

和

hé 1. ...and...
2. harmony

和好 **hé hǎo** reconcile
和氣 **hé qì** amiable; friendly
和平 **hé píng** peace
和事老 **hé shì lǎo** mediator

8 strokes

radical

口

亻	二	千	禾	禾	和	和	和
和	和	和					

媽

mā mother

common words

媽媽　**mā ma**　mother
姨媽　**yí mā**　aunt (mother's married sister)
姑媽　**gū mā**　aunt (father's married sister)

13 strokes

radical
女

simplified form

妈

人	女	女	女	奴	奵	奵	媽
媽	媽	媽	媽	媽	媽	媽	媽

66

哥

gē older brother

common words

哥哥 **gē ge** older brother
大哥 **dà gē** eldest brother
二哥 **èr gē** second elder brother
哥兒們 **gēr men** 1. brothers 2. buddies
帥哥 **shuài gē** handsome man

10 strokes

radical

口

姐

jiě older sister

common words

姐姐 **jiě jie** older sister
姐妹 **jiě mèi** sisters
大姐 **dà jiě** 1. eldest sister 2. older woman
二姐 **èr jiě** second elder sister
小姐 **xiǎo jiě** Miss; lady
空姐 **kōng jiě** air stewardess

弟

dì younger brother

弟弟　**dì di**　younger brother
弟妹　**dì mèi**　1. younger brother and sister 2. younger brother's wife
兄弟　**xiōng dì**　brothers
姐弟　**jiě dì**　older sister and younger brother
徒弟　**tú dì**　disciple; follower

7 strokes

radical
弓

`	`	`	`	`	弟	弟	弟
弟	弟						

69

妹

mèi younger sister

radical
女

common words

妹妹　**mèi mei**　younger sister
大妹　**dà mèi**　first younger sister
三妹　**sān mèi**　third younger sister
小妹　**xiǎo mèi**　youngest sister
姐妹　**jiě mèi**　sisters
兄弟姐妹　**xiōng dì jiě mèi**　brothers and sisters

住	**common words**	**7 strokes**
	住家 **zhù jiā** residence	**radical**
	住址 **zhù zhǐ** address (residence)	人（亻）
zhù 1. live; stay 2. stop	住口 **zhù kǒu** shut up 住手 **zhù shǒu** Hands off! 站住 **zhàn zhù** Halt! 記住 **jì zhù** remember	

亻	亻	亻	仁	住	住	住
住	住					

在

zài 1. be; at 2. live

radical

土

common words

在嗎? **zài ma** in?
在家裡 **zài jiā lǐ** at home
不在 **bú zài** not in
現在 **xiàn zài** now; currently
還在 **hái zài** still there
好在 **hǎo zài** fortunately

一 ナ 不 存 在 在 在

在

這	**common words**	**10 strokes**
	這個 **zhè ge** 1. this one 2. in this case; in this matter	**radical**
	這兒/這裡/這邊 **zhèr/zhè lǐ/zhè biān** here	辵 (辶)
	這些 **zhè xiē** these	**simplified form**
zhè this	這樣 **zhè yàng** this way; like this	
	這麼 **zhè me** such, so	这
	這次 **zhè cì** this time	
	到這兒來 **dào zhèr lái** Come here!	

女

nǚ female

common words

女兒 **nǚ ér** daughter
女生 **nǚ shēng** female student; school girl
女性 **nǚ xìng** female gender
女士 **nǚ shì** Madam
女人 **nǚ rén** 1. woman 2. wife 3. mistress
婦女 **fù nǚ** woman

女 女 女 女

兒

ér/r 1. child 2. suffix

radical

儿

common words

兒子 **ér zi** son
兒童 **ér tóng** child
大兒子 **dà ér zi** eldest son
小兒子 **xiǎo ér zi** youngest son
一會兒 **yí huìr** a moment; a short while
一點兒 **yì diǎnr** a little

simplified form

儿

⺈¹	⺁²	白³	白⁴	白⁵	白⁶	兒⁷	兒⁸
兒	兒	兒					

那

nà/nèi 1. that
2. in that case

radical

邑（右 阝）

common words

那個 **nà ge** that (one)
那裡/那兒/那邊 **nà li/nàr/nà biān** there
那些 **nà xiē** those
那樣 **nà yàng** 1. same as 2. that type
那麼 **nà me** 1. in that case; then 2. same way
那麼點兒 **nà me diǎnr** such a small amount ...

男

nán male

common words

男孩/男孩子 **nán hái/nán hái zi** boy
男生 **nán shēng** male student; school boy
男人 **nán rén** man
男性 **nán xìng** male gender
男男女女 **nán nán nǚ nǚ** boys and girls
男厕/男厕所 **nán cè/nán cè suǒ** man's toilet

丿	冂	日	毌	田	罗	男	男

男	男					

孩

hái child

common words

孩子/小孩 **hái zi/xiǎo hái** child
孩子氣 **hái zi qì** childish
孩子話 **hái zi huà** childish words
男孩/男孩子 **nán hái/nán hái zi** boy
女孩/女孩子 **nǔ hái/nǔ hái zi** girl

9 strokes

radical

子

了　了　子　孖　孖　孩　孩　孩

孩　孩　孩　孩

78

子

zi/zǐ 1. son 2. seed
3. suffix (noun)

common words

子女/兒女 **zǐ nǚ/ér nǚ** son and daughter; children
兒子 **ér zi** son
妻子 **qī zi** wife
桌子 **zhuō zi** table; desk
車子 **chē zi** 1. vehicle (small scale) 2. bicycle
一下子 **yí xià zi** 1. all of a sudden 2. all at once

3 strokes

radical

子

了 子 子 子 子

都

dōu/dū 1. all; even
          2. big city

common words

都有 **dōu yǒu** all have
都是 **dōu shì** all are
都會 **dōu huì** all know how to do
都市/都會 **dū shì/dū huì** big city
首都 **shǒu dū** capital city

radical

邑（右阝）

一	卄	土	耂	耂	者	者	者
者	都	都	都	都			

沒		**common words**				**7 strokes**	
		沒有 **méi yǒu** don't have; haven't				**radical**	
		沒錯 **méi cuò** correct				水（氵）	
		沒問題 **méi wèn tí** no question; no problem					
		沒事 **méi shì** 1. free 2. no problem; alright				**simplified form**	
méi haven't; without		沒關係/沒什麼 **méi guān xi/méi shén me** it doesn't matter				没	
		還沒 **hái méi** not yet					

氵	氵	氵	氵	氵	沒	沒	沒
沒	沒						

有	common words	6 strokes

有的/有些 **yǒu de/yǒu xiē** some
有學問 **yǒu xué wèn** knowledgeable
有點兒 **yǒu diǎnr** a little; somewhat
有沒有(?) **yǒu méi yǒu** 1. did you? 2. whether or not
祇有 **zhǐ yǒu** there's only ...
還有 **hái yǒu** moreover; furthermore

radical
月

yǒu has; have

一	广	大	有	有	有	有	有
有							

做

zuò do; make

11 strokes

common words

做好/做完 **zuò hǎo/zuò wán** finish; complete
做錯 **zuò cuò** do wrongly
做人 **zuò rén** be an upright person
做飯 **zuò fàn** cook a meal
做作業 **zuò zuò yè** do assignment
做工 **zuò gōng** work

radical

人（亻）

事			common words			8 strokes
			事事/每事 **shì shì/měi shì** every matter			radical
			事前 **shì qián** in advance; beforehand			㇆
			事後 **shì hòu** afterwards; after the event			

shì matter

common words

事事/每事 **shì shì/měi shì** every matter
事前 **shì qián** in advance; beforehand
事後 **shì hòu** afterwards; after the event
小事 **xiǎo shì** trivial matter
故事 **gù shì** story
做事 **zuò shì** 1. work 2. deal with matters

一	丅	亏	亐	写	写	写	事
事	事	事					

兩

liǎng two

common words

兩個月　**liǎng ge yuè**　two months
兩百　**liǎng bǎi**　two hundred
兩次　**liǎng cì**　twice
兩樣　**liǎng yàng**　two types; different
兩口子　**liǎng kǒu zi**　a couple; husband and wife
沒兩樣　**méi liǎng yàng**　the same

8 strokes

radical

入

simplified form

两

個

gè most common measure word

common words

個個/每個　**gè gè/měi ge** each one (of something)
個人　**gè rén** individual
個子　**gè zi** body size
兩個門　**liǎng ge mén** two doors
那個　**nà ge** that (one)
這個　**zhè ge** 1. this one 2. in this case; in this matter

10 strokes

radical
人（亻）

simplified form
个

86

多

duō 1. many, much
2. far more

多少(?) **duō shǎo** 1. how many/much? 2. tend to
多大(?) **duō dà** 1. how old(?) 2. how big(?)
多半 **duō bàn** more often than not
多麼 **duō me** no matter how
差不多 **chà bu duō** about; more or less

少

shǎo/shào 1. few; little 2. young

common words

少女　**shào nǚ**　teenage girl
少不了　**shǎo bu liǎo**　can't do without
青少年　**qīng shào nián**　teenager
很少　**hěn shǎo**　very little; very few
不少　**bù shǎo**　quite a lot
男女老少　**nán nǚ lǎo shào**　men, women, young and old

丨　小　小　少　少　少　少

時

shí time

common words

時間 **shí jiān** time
時期 **shí qī** period of time
時時／不時 **shí shí/bù shí** often
一時 **yī shí** temporarily; momentarily
有時／有時候 **yǒu shí/yǒu shí hou** sometimes
到時 **dào shí** when the time comes

10 strokes

radical

日

simplified form

时

丨1	刀2	日3	日4	旷5	旷6	旷7	旷8
時9	時10	時	時	時			

間

jiān 1. between
2. room 3. measure word

common words

時間 **shí jiān** time
中間 **zhōng jiān** between; in the middle
房間 **fáng jiān** room
夜間 **yè jiān** at night; night time
洗手間 **xǐ shǒu jiān** washroom
一間客房 **yī jiān kè fáng** a guest room

12 strokes

radical

門

simplified form

间

今			

jīn now; at present

4 strokes

radical

人（亻）

common words

今天/今日　**jīn tiān/jīn rì** today
今早　**jīn zǎo** this morning
今晚　**jīn wǎn** tonight; this evening
今年　**jīn nián** this year
今後　**jīn hòu** from now on
至今　**zhì jīn** up to now; so far
如今　**rú jīn** now; nowadays

ノ	人	仝	今	今	今	今	

天

tiān 1. day 2. sky

common words

天天/每天 **tiān tiān/měi tiān** every day
天上/天空中 **tiān shàng/tiān kōng zhōng**
in the sky
天氣 **tiān qì** weather
明天 **míng tiān** tomorrow
昨天 **zuó tiān** yesterday
白天 **bái tiān** daytime

幾

jǐ/jī 1. how many
2. several 3. almost

common words

幾個(?) **jǐ ge** 1. how many? 2. several (of something)
幾次(?) **jǐ cì** 1. how many times? 2. several times
幾時(?) **jǐ shí** 1. when? 2. anytime
幾天(?) **jǐ tiān** 1. how many days? 2. several days
幾分(?) **jǐ fēn** 1. how many points? 2. somewhat
幾點(?) **jǐ diǎn** 1. what time? 2. several dots
幾乎 **jī hū** almost, nearly

12 strokes

radical

幺

simplified form

几

	common words				13 strokes		

號

hào 1. date 2. size
3. sequence 4. signal

common words

號碼 **hào mǎ** number
幾號? **jǐ hào** which number?; what size?; what date?
十號 **shí hào** number ten; size ten; tenth (of a month)
句號 **jù hào** full-stop
逗號 **dòu hào** comma
問號 **wèn hào** question mark

13 strokes

radical
虍

simplified form

号

丿¹	²口	口₃	弓₄	号₅	号⁶	号₇	号₈
號₉	號₁₀	號₁₁	號₁₂	號₁₃	號	號	號

明

míng bright

radical
日

common words

明明　**míng míng**　obviously
明白　**míng bai**　understand
明天/明日　**míng tiān/míng rì**　tomorrow
明亮　**míng liàng**　bright
文明　**wén míng**　civilized; civilization
發明　**fā míng**　invent

丨¹	刀²	日³	目⁴	明⁵	明⁶	明⁷	明⁸
明	明	明					

年		**common words**					6 strokes

common words

年年/每年 **nián nián/měi nián** every year
年紀 **nián jì** age
明年 **míng nián** next year
後年 **hòu nián** year after next year
去年 **qù nián** last year
前年 **qián nián** year before last year

nián year

6 strokes

radical

干

common words	4 strokes
月亮/月球 **yuè liang/yuè qiú** moon 月光 **yuè guāng** moonlight 這個月 **zhè ge yuè** this month 上個月 **shàng ge yuè** last month 下個月 **xià ge yuè** next month	radical 月

yuè 1. month 2. moon

丿	刀	月	月	月	月	月

日

rì day

日本　**rì běn**　Japan
日期　**rì qī**　date
日子　**rì zi**　1. date; day 2. time 3. life
今日　**jīn rì**　today
明日　**míng rì**　tomorrow
昨日　**zuó rì**　yesterday
每日　**měi rì**　every day

4 strokes

radical

日

星

xīng star

radical

日

common words

星星 **xīng xing** star
星期 **xīng qī** week
星座 **xīng zuó** 1. constellation 2. sign of zodiac
星球 **xīng qiú** heavenly body; planet
歌星 **gē xīng** singer
明星 **míng xīng** star (celebrity)

星 星 星 星

期

qī period

common words

期間/時期　**qī jiān/shí qī**　period of time
學期　**xué qī**　school term; semester
假期　**jià qī**　holiday
到期　**dào qī**　expire
早期　**zǎo qī**　earlier time; early stage
上星期　**shàng xīng qī**　last week
下星期　**xià xīng qī**　next week

12 strokes

radical

月

一　十　廿　甘　甘　其　其　其

期　期　期　期　期　期　期

100

早	

common words

早安 **zǎo ān** Good morning!

早上 **zǎo shang** morning

早日 **zǎo rì** (at an) early date; soon

早晚 **zǎo wǎn** 1. day and night 2. sooner or later

早飯/早點/早餐 **zǎo fàn/zǎo diǎn/zǎo cān** breakfast

一早 **yī zǎo** early in the morning

明早 **míng zǎo** tomorrow morning

zǎo early; morning; Good morning!

上

shàng 1. above; go up
2. attend 3. previous

radical

一

common words

上面 **shàng mian** above; top
上來 **shàng lái** come up
上去 **shàng qù** go up
上班 **shàng bān** go to work
上廁所 **shàng cè suǒ** go to the toilet
上次 **shàng cì** last time
馬上 **mǎ shàng** immediately

丨 上 上 上 上 上

		common words		3 strokes

下

xià 1. under; go down
    2. finish 3. next

common words

下面 **xià mian** underneath; below
下來 **xià lái** come down
下去 **xià qù** go down
下班 **xià bān** finish work
下雨 **xià yǔ** rain
下次 **xià cì** next time
一下 **yí xià** 1. one time 2. a short while

3 strokes

radical

一

一	下	下	下	下	下		

午

wǔ noon

午飯/午餐 **wǔ fàn/wǔ cān** lunch
午覺/午睡 **wǔ jiào/wǔ shuì** afternoon nap
午夜 **wǔ yè** midnight
上午/午前 **shàng wǔ/wǔ qián** morning (a.m.)
中午 **zhōng wǔ** noon
下午/午後 **xià wǔ/wǔ hòu** afternoon (p.m.)

4 strokes

radical
十

| ノ | 仁 | 仁 | 午 | 午 | 午 | 午 | |

吃

chī eat

吃饭 **chī fàn** have a meal
吃饱了 **chī bǎo le** eaten; eaten enough
吃不饱 **chī bu bǎo** not full; not enough to eat
吃不下 **chī bu xià** not able to eat; have no appetite
小吃 **xiǎo chī** snack
好吃 **hǎo chī** tasty; delicious

6 strokes

radical
口

丨	口	口	叽	吃	吃	吃	吃
吃							

晚

wǎn night; late

common words

晚上 **wǎn shang** evening; night
晚安 **wǎn ān** Good night!
晚飯/晚餐 **wǎn fàn/wǎn cān** dinner
晚班 **wǎn bān** evening shift; night shift
晚點 **wǎn diǎn** be late
起晚了 **qǐ wǎn le** got up late

飯

fàn meal; cooked rice

飯前 **fàn qián** before a meal
飯後 **fàn hòu** after a meal
飯菜 **fàn cài** rice and dishes
飯店 **fàn diàn** 1. restaurant 2. hotel
白飯 **bái fàn** cooked white rice
開飯 **kāi fàn** start serving a meal

12 strokes

radical
食

simplified form
饭

107

了

le/liǎo particle

common words

了不起 **liǎo bu qǐ** fantastic; amazing
對了 **duì le** That's right!
算了 **suàn le** forget it
都上學了 **dōu shàng xué le** all have gone to school
受不了 **shòu bu liǎo** unbearable
吃了 **chī le** had eaten

哪

nǎ/něi which; any

common words

哪個(?) **nǎ ge** 1. which? 2. any; anyone
哪裡(?) **nǎ li** 1. where? 2. not at all
哪樣(?) **nǎ yàng** 1. what kind? 2. whatever
哪天(?) **nǎ tiān** 1. which day? 2. any day; someday
哪些(?) **nǎ xiē** 1. which of those? 2. any of those
哪怕 **nǎ pà** no matter

9 strokes

radical

口

丨	口	口	叮	叧	叧	呀	哪
哪	哪	哪	哪				

Hanyu Pinyin Index

Radical Index

1 stroke

[一]

一	yī	10
七	qī	16
三	sān	12
上	shàng	102
下	xià	103
不	bù	60

[丨]

中	zhōng/zhòng	39

[乙]

九	jiǔ	18
也	yě	59

[丿]

了	le/liǎo	108
事	shì	84

2 strokes

[二]

二	èr	11
五	wǔ	14

人 [亻]

人	rén	57
今	jīn	91
什	shén/shí	30
他	tā	27
你	nǐ	20
住	zhù	71
們	men	50
個	gè	86
做	zuò	83

[儿]

兒	ér/r	75

[入]

兩	liǎng	85

[八]

八	bā	17
六	liù	15

[冂]

再	zài	53

[十]

十	shí	19
午	wǔ	104

[又]

友	yǒu	49

3 strokes

[口]

叫	jiào	29
同	tóng	45
名	míng	32
吃	chī	105
和	hé	65
呢	ne	51
問	wèn	24
哥	gē	67
哪	nǎ/něi	109
嗎	ma	58

[囗]

四	sì	13
國	guó	56

[土]

在	zài	72

[夕]

多	duō	87

[大]

大	dà	36
天	tiān	92

[女]

女	nǚ	74
好	hǎo/háo	22
她	tā	28
姓	xìng	26
妹	mèi	70
姐	jiě	68
媽	mā	66

[子]

子	zi/zǐ	79
字	zì	33
孩	hái	78
學	xué	37

[宀]

家	jiā	63

[小]

小	xiǎo	47
少	shǎo/shào	88

[巾]

師	shī	44

[干]

年	nián	96

[幺]

幾	jǐ/jī	93

[弓]

弟	dì	69

4 strokes
[心]
您   nín   21

[戈]
我   wǒ   34

[文]
文   wén   41

[日]
日   rì   98
早   zǎo   101
明   míng   95
是   shì   35
星   xīng   99
時   shí   89
晚   wǎn   106

[月]
月   yuè   97
有   yǒu   82
朋   péng   48
期   qī   100

[木]
校   xiào   46

水 [氵]
沒   méi   81

[父]
爸   bà   64

5 strokes
[生]
生   shēng   38

[田]
男   nán   77

[白]
的   de   62

6 strokes
羊 [⺶]
美   měi   55

[老]
老   lǎo   43

艸 [艹]
英   yīng   40

[虍]
號   hào   94

7 strokes
[見]
見   jiàn   54

[言]
誰   shéi/shuí   61
請   qǐng   23
課   kè   42
謝   xiè   52

[貝]
貴   guì   25

辵 [辶]
這   zhè   73

邑 [右阝]
那   nà/nèi   76
都   dōu/dū   80

8 strokes
[門]
間   jiān   90

9 strokes
[食]
飯   fàn   107

11 strokes
[麻]
麼   me   31

English–Chinese Index

fortunately 好在 hǎo zài *72*

forty 四十 sì shí *13*

four 四 sì *13*

four hundred 四百 sì bǎi *13*

fourteen 十四 shí sì *13*

fourth 第四 dì sì *13*

free 沒事 méi shì *81*

French (written) 法文 fǎ wén *41*

friend 朋友 péng you *48*; 友人 yǒu rén *49*

friendly 和氣 hé qì *65*

friendship 友誼/友情 yǒu yì/yǒu qíng *49*

Friday 星期五 xīng qī wǔ *14*

from now on 今後 jīn hòu *91*

full name 姓名 xìng míng *26*

full-stop 句號 jù hào *94*

furthermore 還有 hái yǒu *82*

G

gang leader 老大 lǎo dà *43*

gentlemen 男士們 nán shì men *50*

get better (from an illness) 見好 jiàn hǎo *54*

girl 女孩/女孩子 nǔ hái/nǔ hái zi *78*

girlfriend 女朋友 nǔ péng you *48*; 女友 nǔ yǒu *49*

give birth 生 shēng *38*

go abroad 出國 chū guó *56*

go down 下/下去 xià/xià qù *103*

go to school 上學 shàng xué *37*

go to the toilet 上廁所 shàng cè suǒ *102*

go to work 上班 shàng bān *102*

go up 上/上去 shàng/shàng qù *102*

good 好 hǎo *22*

Good! 好啊! hǎo a *22*

good? 好嗎? hǎo ma *58*

good friend 好朋友 hǎo péng you *48*; 好友 hǎo yǒu *49*

good looking 好看 hǎo kàn *22*

Good morning! 您早 nín zǎo *21*; 早/早安 zǎo/zǎo ān *101*

Good night! 晚安 wǎn ān *106*

good show 好看 hǎo kàn *22*

Goodbye! 再見/再會 zài jiàn/zài huì *53*

got up late 起晚了 qǐ wǎn le *106*

great 大 dà *36*

guest 客人 kè rén *57*

H

had eaten 吃了 chī le *108*

Halt! 站住 zhàn zhù *71*

Hands off! 住手 zhù shǒu *71*

handsome 英俊 yīng jùn *40*

handsome man 帥哥 shuài gē *67*

harmony 和 hé *65*

has/have 有 yǒu *82*

have a meal 吃飯 chī fàn *105*

have no appetite 吃不下 chī bu xià *105*

haven't 沒/沒有 méi/méi yǒu *81*

having the same name 同名 tóng míng *32*

having the same surname 同姓 tóng xìng *26*

he 他 tā *27*

hear 聽見 tīng jiàn *54*

heavenly body 星球 xīng qiú *99*

here 這兒/這裡/這邊 zhèr/zhè lǐ/zhè biān *73*

hero 英/英雄 yīng/yīng xióng *40*

hers 她的 tā de *28, 62*

his 他的 tā de *27, 62*

hit by (an arrow) 中 zhòng *39*

hobby, interest in something 愛好 ài hào *22*

holiday 假期 jià qī *100*

home 家 jiā *63*

homework 功課 gōng kè *42*

honorable 貴 guì *25*

hotel 飯店 fàn diàn *107*

hour 小時 xiǎo shí *47*

how 怎麼 zěn me *31*

How about him/her? 他(她)呢? tā ne *51*

How about us? 我們呢? wǒ men ne *51*

How about you? 你呢? nǐ ne *51*

how big(?) 多大(?) duō dà *87*

How do you do? 你好 nǐ hǎo *20*

How do you do? (polite) 您好 nín hǎo *21*

how many 幾 jǐ *93*

how many (of something)? 幾個? jǐ ge *93*

how many/much(?) 多少(?) duō shǎo *87*

number nine 九號 jiǔ hào *18*
number ten 十號 shí hào *94*

O

obviously 明明 míng míng *95*
October 十月 shí yuè *19*
often 時時/不時 shí shí/bù shí *89*
OK! 好啊! hǎo a *22*
old 老 lǎo *43*
old friend 老朋友 lǎo péng you *48*
old woman 老婆婆 lǎo pó po *43*
older brother 哥/哥哥 gē/gē ge *67*
older sister 姐/姐姐 jiě/jiě jie *68*
older sister and younger brother 姐弟 jiě dì *69*
older woman 大姐 dà jiě *68*
on hand 手中 shǒu zhōng *39*
once 一次 yí cì *10*
once more 再次 zài cì *53*
one 一 yī *10*
one (of something) 一個 yí ge *10*
one time 一下 yí xià *103*
oneself 本人 běn rén *57*
or 還是 hái shì *35*
or/or else 再不 zài bu *53*
order 叫 jiào *29*
order a cab 叫車 jiào chī *29*
other 其他 qí tā *27*
other people 他人/其他人 tā rén/qí tā rén *27*
other people 人家 rén jiā *63*
our country 我國 wǒ guó *34*

P

parents 爸爸媽媽 bà ba mā ma *64*
particle 的 de *62*; 了 le/liǎo *108*
peace 和平 hé píng *65*
people 人們 rén men *50*
people of a country 國民 guó mín *56*
people from another country, foreigners 外國人 wài guó rén *56*
perfect 十全十美 shí quán shí měi *19*
perhaps 也許 yě xǔ *59*

period of time 時期 shí qī *89, 100*; 期間 qī jiān *100*
person/people 人 rén *57*
planet 星球 xīng qiú *99*
play host 請客 qǐng kè *23*
please 請 qǐng *23*
Please come in. 請進 qǐng jìn *23*
Please sit down. 請坐 qǐng zuò *23*
plural suffix (for persons) 們 men *50*
population 人口 rén kǒu *57*
pretty 美麗 měi lì *55*
previous 上 shàng *102*
primary school 小學 xiǎo xué *37*
principal 校長 xiào zhǎng *46*
probably 大概 dà gài *36*
problem 問題 wèn tí *24*
proud 自大 zì dà *36*

Q

question 問題 wèn tí *24*
question and answer 問答 wèn dá *24*
question mark 問號 wèn hào *94*
question particle 呢 ne *51*; 嗎 ma *58*
quite a lot 不少 bù shǎo *88*
quite good 挺好的 tǐng hǎo de *62*

R

rain 下雨 xià yǔ *103*
rare 少見 shǎo jiàn *54*
raw 生 shēng *38*
reconcile 和好 hé hǎo *65*
related to England 英 yīng *40*
remember 記住 jì zhù *71*
repeatedly 再三/一再 zài sān/yí zài *53*
residence 住家 zhù jiā *71*
respected person 貴人 guì rén *25*
restaurant 飯店 fàn diàn *107*
return home 回家 huí jiā *63*
rice and dishes 飯菜 fàn cài *107*
room 間/房間 jiān/fáng jiān *90*

List of Radicals

— 1 stroke —

1	一	one
2	丨	down
3	、	dot
4	丿	left
5	乙	twist
6	亅	hook

— 2 strokes —

7	二	two
8	亠	lid
9	人	man
10	儿	legs
11	入	enter
12	八	eight
13	冂	borders
14	冖	crown
15	冫	ice
16	几	table
17	凵	bowl
18	刀	knife
19	力	strength
20	勹	wrap
21	匕	ladle
22	匚	basket
23	匸	box
24	十	ten
25	卜	divine
26	卩	seal
27	厂	slope
28	厶	cocoon
29	又	right hand

— 3 strokes —

30	口	mouth
31	囗	surround
32	土	earth
33	士	knight
34	夂	follow
35	夊	slow
36	夕	dusk
37	大	big
38	女	woman
39	子	child
40	宀	roof
41	寸	thumb
42	小	small
43	尢	lame
44	尸	corpse
45	屮	sprout
46	山	mountain
47	川	river
48	工	work
49	己	self
50	巾	cloth
51	干	shield
52	幺	coil
53	广	lean-to
54	廴	march
55	廾	clasp
56	弋	dart
57	弓	bow

— 4 strokes —

58	彐	pig's head
59	彡	streaks
60	彳	step
61	心	heart
62	戈	lance
63	戶	door
64	手	hand
65	支	branch
66	攴	knock
67	文	pattern
68	斗	peck
69	斤	axe
70	方	square
71	无	lack
72	日	sun
73	曰	say
74	月	moon
75	木	tree
76	欠	yawn
77	止	toe
78	歹	chip
79	殳	club
80	毋	don't
81	比	compare
82	毛	fur
83	氏	clan
84	气	breath
85	水	water
86	火	fire
87	爪	claws
88	父	father
89	爻	crisscross
90	爿	bed
91	片	slice
92	牙	tooth
93	牛	cow
94	犬	dog

— 5 strokes —

95	玄	dark
96	玉	jade
97	瓜	melon
98	瓦	tile
99	甘	sweet
100	生	birth
101	用	use
102	田	field
103	疋	bolt
104	疒	sick
105	癶	back
106	白	white
107	皮	skin
108	皿	dish
109	目	eye
110	矛	spear
111	矢	arrow
112	石	rock
113	示	sign
114	禸	track
115	禾	grain

— 6 strokes —

116	穴	cave
117	立	stand
118	竹	bamboo
119	米	rice
120	糸	silk
121	缶	crock
122	网	net
123	羊	sheep
124	羽	wings
125	老	old
126	而	beard
127	耒	plow
128	耳	ear
129	聿	brush
130	肉	meat
131	臣	bureaucrat
132	自	small nose
133	至	reach
134	臼	mortar
135	舌	tongue
136	舛	discord
137	舟	boat
138	艮	stubborn
139	色	color
140	艸	grass
141	虍	tiger
142	虫	bug
143	血	blood
144	行	go
145	衣	gown
146	襾	cover

— 7 strokes —

147	見	see
148	角	horn
149	言	words
150	谷	valley
151	豆	flask
152	豕	pig
153	豸	snake
154	貝	cowrie
155	赤	red
156	走	walk
157	足	foot
158	身	torso
159	車	car
160	辛	bitter
161	辰	early
162	辵	halt
163	邑	city
164	酉	wine
165	釆	sift
166	里	village

— 8 strokes —

167	金	gold
168	長	long
169	門	gate
170	阜	mound
171	隶	grab
172	隹	dove
173	雨	rain
174	青	green
175	非	wrong

— 9 strokes —

176	面	face
177	革	hide
178	韋	walk off
179	韭	leeks
180	音	tone
181	頁	head
182	風	wind
183	飛	fly
184	食	food
185	首	chief
186	香	scent

— 10 strokes —

187	馬	horse
188	骨	bone
189	高	tall
190	髟	hair
191	鬥	fight
192	鬯	mixed wine
193	鬲	cauldron
194	鬼	ghost

— 11 strokes —

195	魚	fish
196	鳥	bird
197	鹵	salt
198	鹿	deer
199	麥	wheat
200	麻	hemp

— 12 strokes —

201	黃	yellow
202	黍	millet
203	黑	black
204	黹	embroider

— 13 strokes —

205	黽	toad
206	鼎	tripod
207	鼓	drum
208	鼠	mouse

— 14 strokes —

209	鼻	big nose
210	齊	line-up

— 15 strokes —

211	齒	teeth

— 16 strokes —

212	龍	dragon
213	龜	tortoise

— 17 strokes —

214	龠	flute